CONTENTS

Introduction

INTRODUCTION

One of the aims of pre-school settings is to promote young children's learning and development and pre-school workers play a crucial role in enabling pre-schools to achieve this aim.

This book offers help and advice to pre-school workers about an important aspect of promoting children's learning and development. That is, the evidence collection, assessment, recording and planning needed to ensure that the provision of each pre-school setting promotes the learning and development of each child.

The first chapter looks at what is involved in planning the curriculum of a pre-school setting and why it is essential for this to be based on knowledge of individual children.

Chapters 2 reviews the types of evidence that can be gathered to provide information about individual children's interests, activities and behaviours. Chapter 3 looks at observation as a source of evidence. It introduces a range of methods for observing children and considers the type of information that each method provides.

Once pre-school workers have collected evidence about children's interests, activities and behaviours they need to analyse it to assess children's levels of achievement. Chapter 4 looks at how to do this.

In order to be able to use these assessments in future planning, pre-schools need to keep records of children's achievements and chapter 5 looks at how to keep such records.

Chapter 6 covers the use of assessments of children's levels of achievement to create individual plans which set out how their learning is to be progressed.

We emphasise throughout the book that there is no single correct way to collect evidence, keep records and set out plans to progress children's learning. Each pre-school setting needs to find a way that is manageable and enables the setting to promote children's learning and development effectively. We have given examples of ways which pre-schools have found to be helpful. The Appendices contain proformas for a range of methods of gathering and recording information that can be photocopied.

This material will be of value not only to pre-school workers but also to other early years professionals and to students on Level 2 or Level 3 courses such as the CACHE Certificate in Pre-school Practice and the CACHE Diploma in Pre-school Practice.

Working in partnership with children's parents is an important part of best practice in pre-school settings. As we introduce each part of the process of providing a curriculum that progresses the learning of individual children, we consider how staff and parents can work together. we also consider how children can contribute to the process of planning for their own learning.

A commitment to quality by pre-school settings involves them in providing a curriculum that meets the needs of each child. These needs change as she/he learns and develops. In order to meet the needs of each child, pre-school settings must be aware of and respond to these changes. This will involve settings in continuous cycles of evidence collection, assessment, recording, planning and implementing the plans. The place where each cycle starts is with the child.

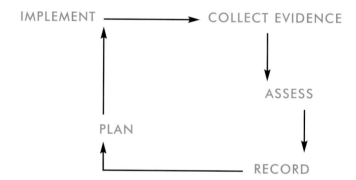

CHAPTER 1 - THE NEEDS OF CHILDREN

One morning, the staff at ABC Pre-school are preparing the water tray for the arrival of the children. It is the policy in the setting to have the water available to the children in some form throughout the session and, as they put out the equipment, the staff think about some of the children who may be using it during the course of the day:

■ *Jack, who is at the very beginning of learning to share equipment and resources with other children*

■ *Daniel, who is fascinated by anything to do with boats*

■ *Eva, whose hand and arm muscle control enable her to pour from containers such as cups and large jugs*

■ *Anouk, who brings up and down movements into many of his play activities both at home and in the pre-school, and was very excited last week by the way coloured water could be made to go up and down a tube by means of a siphon*

■ *Gracie, who can recite the numbers one to ten in the correct order, and is working on counting by relating numbers to objects on a one-to-one basis.*

Given the different interests and stages of progress of these children - and of the other children in the pre-school - how should the staff present the water? What equipment should they put out with it? What specific water-based activities should they plan? How might the staff interact with the children? When they have made all these decisions, how will they know whether their decisions were the right ones?

All pre-schools face such questions, every day, in everything they do.

The information about Jack, Daniel, Eva, Anouk and Gracie demonstrates that each child is an individual. Each child:

■ comes to the setting bringing with them a range of experiences, interests and achievements

■ progresses at different rates in different areas of learning and development

■ is motivated by different things from other children, and by different things at different times.

All children have an equal right to receive in their pre-school setting the support and stimuli they need to enable them to progress. Adults must therefore make appropriate plans for each child's learning. The only way they can do this is by finding out how far each child has progressed and using this as the basis for deciding what she/he should go on to next. The staff in ABC Pre-school have a fund of information and understanding about the individual children in the setting. All staff, in all settings, need such information and understanding, so that they can help to progress the learning and development of each child.

The way to find out about children's progress is to gather information about their interests, activities and behaviour. If pre-school settings are to be able to help all the children in the setting to progress, information must be gathered about all of them. This is not because the children are perceived as a 'problem', or because they are 'special', but because they all have an equal right, as members of the group, to a curriculum that caters appropriately for their individual needs.

Collecting evidence about individual children provides information that can be compared with the expected milestones for children's learning and development. It can then be used to assess each child's stage of progress and to identify the next steps for this progess. In the case of ABC Pre-school, evidence showed that Gracie could recite the number names to ten in the correct order. Comparing this information with the stages of learning involved in developing an understanding of number showed that the next step for her learning should be the ability to count objects one by one using the correct number name as each object is counted. In order to help Gracie to achieve this next step, the pre-school needs to identify appropriate activities to provide her with.

The target for Gracie's development of an understanding of number and the activities to help her to achieve it will form part of her individual learning plan. Information from Gracie's individual learning plan, as well as from those of all of the other children, will need to be used when developing the curriculum plans for the whole pre-school.

The details of how to create long-term, medium and short-term plans are described more fully in other Pre-school Learning Alliance publications. For funded nursery settings, the long-term plan for the setting will need to take account of the early learning goals set by the Qualifications and Curriculum Authority for the end of the Foundation Stage. The medium and short-term plans are informed by the requirements of the long-term plan and by the learning plans of individual children. Thus, the medium and short-term plans will change and develop with the children.

The collection of evidence and its assessment to identify the stages of children's learning and development is the basis for creating individual learning plans which set out the next steps in each child's learning and development. As these plans are implemented, further evidence will need to be gathered and analysed to assess whether children are making progress and, if they are progressing, to identify new targets for their learning and development.

If pre-school staff involve children's parents in this cycle of evidence collection, assessment, planning and implementation, the process can include information about children's interests, activities, behaviours and achievements at home. Without this the picture of their development will be incomplete. It will also mean that parents can complement the activities provided by the pre-school to promote children's learning and development with further activities at home.

Because ongoing evidence collection is an integral part of the work of all pre-school settings, it is important for each pre-school to develop manageable systems for collecting this evidence.

Gathering evidence

CHAPTER 2 - GATHERING EVIDENCE

Nicky, aged 3 years 11 months, is at the painting easel. Kevin, one of the helpers, notices as he passes that instead of swirling a succession of colours all over the paper until it turns brown and gets a hole in the middle, which is what Nicky usually does, she has this time painted separate blocks of colour and has not painted over them. Kevin tells Nicky that he likes the colours in her painting and she says, "It's a pattern." Kevin admires her painting again and suggests that he dates it, writes on it that Nicky said that it was a pattern and asks her to put it in her file.

Kevin is not Nicky's keyworker and is not, therefore, responsible for ensuring that evidence about her progress is collected and analysed. However, he knows that he has a part to play in gathering evidence about all the children, not just those for whom he is the keyworker. This is why he dated Nicky's painting, noted that she said that it was a pattern and suggested to her that she should put it in her file. He knows that Nicky's keyworker will use the information gained from the painting together with other kinds of evidence, when reviewing Nicky's individual learning plan.

The dated example of Nicky's work, which her painting provided, is one example of the evidence that pre-school settings need to collect about each child to assess, record and plan for her/his progress. This evidence should be kept in a record file and might include:

- formal observations of the child
- informal notes on skills/understanding newly demonstrated by the child, such as cutting along a line or counting objects to three, using one to one correspondence between the objects and the correct number names
- the results of tasks set to check the child's skill/understanding in one specific area - pre-schools sometimes set up such tasks to check on aspects of children's learning and development about which everyday activities are unlikely to provide evidence. For example, a pre-school setting might set up an adult initiated activity that tells the staff which children can stand on one leg
- examples of the child's work
- in areas where the child's work does not have an end product, such as role play or climbing, or where the end product cannot be kept, such as building with wooden blocks, dated accounts, sketches, photographs or videos
- tape recordings of the child's conversations
- information from parents about the child's activities and interests at home
- reports/information from any other professionals working with the child, including speech or other therapists.

The evidence collected about children's activities and behaviours can make an invaluable contribution when a child is being assessed with a view to receiving a Statement of Special Educational Needs under the Children Act 1989 or the Education Act 2001. They will show how a child has developed over a period of time and can help to pinpoint areas of delay. The record can support health professionals, educational psychologists and other professionals in building up as complete a picture as possible of the child's needs. This holistic picture, developed over time and in a context familiar to the child, can form a reliable basis for making decisions about individual education plans and about levels of support needed. It can also support the parents' contribution to the statementing process.

Evidence provides the basis for assessment, record keeping and planning and its implementation. As a result, the quality of the evidence used by pre-school workers is key to providing effectively for children's learning and development.

The quality of evidence

A pre-school setting can be confident that the evidence it collects about each child is good quality, if it is

- objective
- unbiased
- not distorted
- collected systematically
- consistent
- appropriate.

Objective

Evidence is objective if it provides information about what a child actually did or said. It is not objective, if it includes an interpretation by the person collecting the evidence of what the child said or did.

Anyone recording a formal or informal observation of a child needs to take particular care that what they write is objective.

An adult making an objective observation of a child might record "*Holding a large brush in his left hand, Joe dips the brush in the red paint and paints two vertical strokes. He dips the brush in the blue pot and makes two horizontal strokes, joining up the first two into a square. He dips the brush into the black paint and puts a short black vertical line on top of the square.*"

If the adult making the observation recorded, "*Joe paints a house with a chimney*", the observation would not be objective, because this is an adult interpretation of what Joe has done. If Joe talked about his painting, and said, "*It's a house*" this should be recorded.

Evidence about children's social development will not be objective if judgements about their interactions with one another are recorded. If Katie rushes up to Darren and gives him a push, this is what the observer should record, not that she was aggressive towards him. If pushing other children is a common feature of evidence about Katie's interactions with other children, the pre-school setting will want to investigate this and to check whether it is preventing other children from approaching Katie.

Unbiased

The evidence that is collected about each child needs to provide a full and complete picture of what children are saying and doing. The adults responsible for collecting this evidence have to be aware constantly of the danger of making unwarranted and stereotyped assumptions. These can prevent adults from seeing what is really there because they have already decided what they expected to see. For example, a keyworker may have noted that a particular child is unwilling to join group storytelling sessions and often tries to leave them. On the basis of this, the keyworker may have decided that the child does not like books and so have failed to notice that the child does spend time in the book corner looking at books on her own.

Stereotypical assumptions about children's activities and behaviour based on their gender can be another source of bias in the gathering of evidence. For example, assuming that only boys are interested in games involving kicking may result in an activity set up to provide evidence about children's ability to kick not including any girls.

Not distorted

It can be hard to behave naturally or spontaneously while obviously being watched by someone else. Children can become inhibited if they know they are being watched and this may result in them doing less than they are capable of. Another response, which children sometimes make whilst being watched is to put on a 'public performance' by behaving in ways they think the watching adult expects or will approve of. In either case, the resulting observation will not give reliable information about how the child normally behaves or what she/he can do. The evidence collector needs to be as unobtrusive as possible. Helpful techniques include:

- making all children familiar with the fact that notes will sometimes be taken about the pre-school and what is done there
- avoiding conversation as far as possible with children who are being observed
- sitting/crouching sideways to children who are being observed to get as close as possible whilst avoiding eye contact
- observing for a short while before taking notes and then pausing for another period before taking notes again
- explaining what the tape recorder is being used for and give children opportunities to get used to its presence, before using it to record evidence of children's conversations
- positioning yourself so that you do not attract the children's attention when using cameras and video-recorders
- introducing, in a relaxed way as if it were any other adult-initiated activity, a specific task to check children's skill/understanding.

Collected systematically

The evidence collected by pre-school settings about each of the children should help to build up an all round picture of what the children know and can do. Consequently, it must be collected regularly and checked to make sure that it is providing information about children's activity and behaviour in each of the areas of learning and development. Someone in the pre-school setting will need to take responsibility for ensuring that this happens. In many pre-schools, it is the keyworkers who ensure that evidence about the children for whom they are responsible is collected and checked regularly.

Pre-schools can help their staff with evidence collection by introducing a system of informal note-taking about the activities/skills/understanding demonstrated by children during the pre-school session. For example, staff might carry a pad of post-it notes in their pockets at each session, or printed proformas could be readily available where all staff can access them quickly. A proforma is included in Appendix 1.

Sometimes, it is not possible to make an informal note of a child's actions at the exact time the event takes place. However, the actions should be noted down as soon as possible after the event because memory is not always reliable, especially in a busy pre-school session.

All pieces of evidence should include the date on which it was collected. This is important in putting together a picture of children's progress. If a piece of evidence is not going to be placed into a child's record file straightaway, the child's name should also be noted on it. Sometimes, it will be helpful to add a brief note of the background circumstances to a piece of evidence. For example, noting whether the child was playing on her/his own, with other children or with an adult present, will give an indication of how the child behaves in different social contexts.

Consistent

A single piece of evidence is never enough by itself. Especially, if it seems to indicate something new or surprising about a child, it is important to look for further evidence that confirms the finding. In the example at the beginning of this chapter, Nicky's keyworker would need to look for further evidence that Nicky was producing paintings with blocks of colour to be able to say that she had reached the stage of producing patch paintings. When a piece of evidence has shown something new about a child, it will alert staff and the child's parents to look out for further evidence to support it.

Paired observation can be a useful way to check on the consistency of the evidence provided by formal observation methods. An observer who wants to be sure of the validity of what she/he has observed might ask another adult to observe the same child or activity and then to compare notes.

Appropriate

Different types of evidence collection are appropriate in different circumstances. This is particularly true of formal observations. The next chapter examines a range of observation methods, and it is important to choose the right one for the purpose. For example, if you want to know whether a child is developing independence in selecting and using activities, you should use an observation designed to show the range of activities a child uses during the course of the session and what causes the child to move from one activity to another. If, however, you want to know about a child's ability to use a tool, such as scissors, you would use a descriptive observation of her/him at an activity that involves using scissors.

The role of the adults

Collecting evidence is something to which all the adults involved with the pre-school setting can contribute. There are several reasons for this:

- evidence is validated by coming from a range of sources
- evidence collection, like planning, is an ongoing responsibility, and can be done more thoroughly if there are more people to share it
- there needs to be a commitment by the whole group to the cycle of evidence collection-recording-assessment-planning and implementation. Without commitment there is a danger that it can be seen, not as a tool to make the provision effective for the children, but as a burden, an intrusion or even a threat
- pooled resources are more powerful and more comprehensive. A child's current interest in a particular activity or idea cannot be picked up by a single observation. It takes input from many people, and from the child's home as well as the pre-school setting, to recognise a pattern in children's behaviour. In the case study at the beginning of the chapter, Nicky said her painting was a pattern. Her keyworker might decide to ask other members of staff to try to note whether Nicky brings pattern-making into other activities. By talking to Nicky's parents, the keyworker may find that they have noticed that she is fascinated by the patterns of the bricks in walls and the paving stones in the pavements.

For all these reasons, all the adults in the pre-school setting need to be aware of the setting's systems for evidence collection, and of the ways in which each adult can make a contribution.

Parents

Parents are the prime source of knowledge about their own child. This knowledge is an important part of the evidence the pre-school setting needs to construct an accurate picture of the child's interests, activities, experiences and achievements. Pre-school settings need to find ways to enable each child's parents and the pre-school staff to exchange their knowledge about the children. To make it easy for all parents to make an input in this way, it is important for each setting to create systems that allow regular and frequent opportunities for parents to share information and insights about their own children. Such systems can include:

- informal conversations with keyworkers at the beginning and/or end of sessions
- open days or evenings where parents and staff can have more formal discussions about children's activities
- letting parents know that they can make arrangements, at times convenient to them, to talk with their child's keyworker
- giving parents access to their own child's record file, so that they can add evidence from children's activities at home and see the evidence about children's activities in the pre-school setting
- having a 'Home - Pre-school Link' book for each child. This is taken home with examples of the child's work and some brief notes on the child's activities during the week and is returned at the beginning of the following week with results from and notes about the child's activities at home.

Sharing with parents the areas of learning and development in the Foundation Stage, and the early learning goals and the stepping stones for each area will help parents to understand how the evidence about their child can be used to build up a picture of her/his progress in each area.

The exchange of information between parents and pre-school staff and parents' involvement in collecting evidence about their children's progress can make an important contribution to enabling pre-school settings to work in partnership with children's parents.

Keyworkers

Keyworkers will ensure that evidence about the progress of the children for whom they are responsible is collected regularly and that there are opportunities for the children's parents to contribute. Keyworkers will make sure that the evidence is comprehensive, that is, that it provides information about the children's progress in all the areas of learning and development and that there is sufficient evidence to make valid assessments of the children's progress. In addition, they will be alert to any opportunities for making contributions to the evidence gathered on children in other keyworker groups.

Other staff and volunteers

It is important for pre-schools to ensure that all staff and volunteers understand the part that evidence collection plays in promoting the learning and development of individual children. Staff and volunteers also need to be alerted to what they should be looking out for. Sometimes some brief notes on the session plan can be helpful. For example, the session plan of Nicky's pre-school could have a note to look for examples of Nicky creating patterns and it would include similar notes about other children.

Pre-school leaders

In addition to making their own contributions to evidence collection in the setting, leaders will be responsible for initiating discussions and making decisions about the implementation of the setting's evidence collection systems, and for ensuring that the assessments of the evidence feed into the planning and implementation of the setting's curriculum.

Leaders will need to ensure that the pre-school's systems include regular evidence collection and analysis to assess the stages of progress for each child in the setting.

Committees/owners

If staff are to make a full commitment to ongoing evidence collection, assessment and record-keeping, and to using the results as a basis for planning, those responsible for employing staff may need to give serious consideration to the following implications:

- staff and volunteers may need training including training in time management skills
- it may be necessary to allow more non-contact time, with pay, for staff carrying time-consuming responsibilities for conducting and co-ordinating these activities.

Observation Methods

CHAPTER 3 - OBSERVATION METHODS

Sunshine Pre-school uses observations as one of its methods for collecting evidence about the progress of individual children's learning and development. In choosing which methods to use, thought is given to the type of information required about a child at any particular time.

Justin has recently started at the pre-school. It is decided that a narrative observation will provide information about his general development and how he is responding to the activities in the pre-school. The narrative observation shows that he visits most of the available activities spending a short time watching the children using the activity. A week later Justin's keyworker decides to follow up the narrative observation with a tracking observation to see whether he is still using the play activities in the way which the narrative observation revealed.

Formal observations are one of the methods that can be used to collect evidence about children's activities and behaviours.

There are many ways of carrying out observations. None of them is perfect for all situations. Each has its own merits and disadvantages, and each serves a different purpose. When choosing which observation method to use, it is helpful to think of the finished observation as providing the pre-school worker with an answer to a question. In order to get the right answer, it is necessary first is to be clear about what the question is. When deciding which observation method to use, pre-school workers should ask themselves:

1. What do we want to find out about the child's learning and development?
2. Which method of observing will be most likely to provide that information?

This chapter describes a number of approaches to observation, indicating the advantages and disadvantages of each. Before using any unfamiliar method, it is a good idea for staff to practise using the system in advance. Ideally, more than one person should attempt each observation. When a 'paired' observation has taken place, time should then be made for comparing notes, so that any problems or inconsistencies are identified at once and everyone has the opportunity to become confident about using the system.

Narrative observations

These aim to tell the whole 'learning story ' of a particular situation, over a specific period of time. They can be either child-based - following, for the specified period, the movements and behaviour of one child - or activity-based - looking, for the specified period, at a particular activity. Within that framework, there is no pre-selection on the part of the observer. The observation target is the most ambitious possible: no less than everything! The observer aims to record:

■ the circumstances of the observations (the activity, the position in the playroom, the time of day, the equipment available)
■ what is done
■ what is said
■ the social context (the number of people present and their interactions with one another)

Target Child

?79 the Oxford Pre-school Research Group produced a systematic guide to narrative observation of children at play. Because it was designed to focus on the activity of a single child, it became known as the 'Target Child' system .

This method offers a 'shorthand' which enables the observer to record and analyse bulky and complex material both rapidly and systematically. Like any other shorthand, it has to be learned. Once the observer is familiar with the technique, however, the whole task of narrative observation becomes much easier. An additional advantage is that the observations can be shared, if confidentiality allows, with other people. The coded observations will carry the same messages to others who know the system as they did to the writer.

The basic premises are simple ones:

- Observations are recorded on a standard sheet (see Appendix 2) for up to 10 consecutive minutes
- The sheet has columns for recording activity and language
- Everything done by the child who is the subject of the observation, and other relevant people, is recorded in the activity column
- What is said by and to the child is entered, as far as possible, in the language column. Where speech is too rapid or indistinct for this to be possible, the gist of the conversation is entered in brackets
- The child who is the subject of the observations is TC (Target Child)
- Any other child is C
- Any adult is A
- Arrows indicate the direction of interactions. For example:

A	▶	TC	Shall I help you off with your apron?
TC	▶	A	No, I want to do another painting
TC	▶	C	(About who can use the yellow paint)

The record in the activity and language columns is then analysed using a Social Code and Task Code. The results are recorded in the Social and Task columns.

- The Social Code indicates whether, during that minute, the child was:
   Solitary SOL
   with one other person, child or adult PAIR
   in a small group of children (3-6) SG
   in a large group of children (6+) LG

- If the child being observed was in the company of other people but not interacting with them, just pursuing his/her activities beside them, the social code has /P (for parallel) added to it. For example:

   If the child was playing alongside another at the sand tray but was making no contact with the other child, the Social Code would be PAIR/P

The people who produced this system were researchers Kathy Sylva, Marjorie Painter and Carolyn Roy, with suggestions from Linnet McMahon, Martha Kempton and Terry End.

■ If an adult was very close to the child, or interacting with the child in any way, the Social Code is ringed. For example:

> If the child was chatting to an adult with two other children, the Social Code is ⓈⒼ

Sometimes approximations have to be made. If the child spends most of any given minute absorbed in a puzzle, for example, breaking off only briefly to chat to another child, the coding will indicate how the major part of the time was spent and would be SOL.

The presence of an adult, however, is so important and makes such a difference to the quality of play that it should always be recorded. If the child engaged in the puzzle has a brief word with a passing adult, the Social Code will be ⓈⓄⓁ

The Task Code analyses the kind of activity the child was primarily engaged in at the time of the observation.

These are the Task Codes:

LMM (Large muscle movement) - active movement of the child's body, involving co-ordination of larger muscles.

LSC (Large scale construction) - using big blocks, crates, etc: arranging/building dens, trains, etc.

SSC (Small scale construction) - the use of small construction materials: Lego, Sticklebricks, and also nailing things together

ART Child-directed creative activities: painting, cutting, sticking, drawing

MAN (Manipulation) - developing/extending manual skills involving physical co-ordination: handling dough, clay, water etc and arranging, sorting, gardening, sewing.

ADM (Adult directed art and manipulation) - developing skills and techniques under adult direction, sometimes with an adult-directed end product: tracing, directed collage.

SM (Structured materials) - using materials with design constraints: pegboards, jigsaw puzzles, templates, picture/shape matching materials, sewing cards

3Rs ('Three Rs' activities) - attempting to read, write or count: includes attentive looking at books

EX (Examination) - closely examining an object or material, where the looking, smelling, tasting is more important than the manipulation involved: using a nature viewer, examining the effect of a magnet on iron filings.

PS (Problem solving) - solving a problem in a purposeful way using logical reasoning: looking to see why something won't work, then repairing it.

PRE (Pretend) - transforming everyday objects, people or events so that their 'meaning' takes precedence over the 'reality': using a row of chairs as a 'train'.

SVT   (Scale version toys) - arranging miniature objects such as dolls' houses, farm and zoo sets, transport toys, toy forts: not prams, dishes or ordinary dolls; miniature items used for general pretend purposes are coded PRE.

IG   (Informal games) - playing an informal game, with or without language, with another child: spontaneously and loosely organised activities such as following one another around while chanting, hiding in a corner and giggling or holding hands and jumping.

GWR   (Games with rules) - playing rule-governed games: ball games, skittles, circle and singing games, board games, dominoes, noughts & crosses.

MUS   (Music) - responding to sounds, rhythms or music: listening, playing instruments, singing solos, dancing.

PALGA   (Passive, adult led group activities) - listening to stories, watching a video/TV, watching a planned demonstration, all in a large group under the leadership of an adult.

SINP   (Social interaction, non-play) - interacting with another child or with an adult in a way which is not play and does not accompany a play activity: chatting, borrowing, seeking/giving help or information, being aggressive, teasing, being cuddled/comforted by an adult.

DB   (Distress behaviour) - visibly seeking comfort or attention from an adult or another child: prolonged crying, wanton destruction of materials, social withdrawal.

SA/AWG   (Standing around, aimless wander or gaze) - not actively engaged in a task or in watching a specific event.

CR   (Cruise) - moving actively from one thing to another or purposeful looking around: searching for something to do.

PM   (Purposeful movement) - moving deliberately towards a specific object, person or place: looking for something, going outside, crossing to another activity.

W   (Wait) - inactivity while waiting for adult or child: waiting for other children to finish their milk.

WA   (Watching) - watching a specific person or activity, looking around, listening to conversations without participating

DA   (Domestic activity) - hand-washing, dressing, arrival & departure, rest, tidying-up, going to the toilet, having milk, a snack or a meal.

In addition to coding the child's activities and interactions, this observation method can also be used to identify themes - continuous streams of activity. At the end of each theme, a double line is drawn across the observation sheet. A child might spend some time using large blocks to act out the train journey in a story, which had just been read to the children. This would have the Task Code PRE. The child may then use the sticking activity to make a train with the small boxes. This would be Task Code ART. Both activities would contribute to a theme of recalling the train journey in the story.

The completed observation sheet that follows on page 24 will illustrate the way the codes are used, and there is a pro-forma in the Appendix 2 that can be photocopied for use with this system.

The target child observation sheet, once completed, can give access to a lot of information:

■ the level of the child's skills
■ whom the child talks to, in what way and for what purpose
■ themes or activities the child chooses to pursue
■ the length of time the child sustains one theme or activity
■ the amount and level of interaction with other children and with adults, and whether the child initiates it or merely responds
■ whether the child chooses one kind of play, perhaps to the exclusion of others
■ the level of the child's competence in different areas of learning and development
■ the child's current preoccupations, perhaps following through a particular intellectual concept such as the idea of things being 'inside' or 'underneath' one another, or seeking stories, conversations and make-believe play with dolls and other activities which will help express the feelings aroused by a new baby at home.

The observation sheets used for the Target Child method can also be adapted for use as activity-based narrative observations. When observing for this purpose, all children become C, just as all adults are A, and the Task and Social Codes describe the actions and interactions of the majority of the children at the activity under observation.

Activity-based observations of this kind can be a very useful tool for a group wishing to find out whether a particular activity is helping children to achieve the intended outcomes for their learning and development.

A series of observations can reveal:

■ The kinds of play and learning most often promoted by that activity
■ The kinds and quantity of conversation the activity generates
■ Whether the presence of an adult makes a difference to the play and/or conversation
■ Whether the activity lends itself to long stretches of play linked to a single theme or to a series of short, 'one-off' actions
■ What it is that triggers and sustains children's interest and concentration - and what brings them to an end.

Armed with this information, a group is in a good position not only to initiate changes, if they think it necessary, but also to monitor the effects of change.

What the 'Target Child' system offers:

■ Opportunities to gather comprehensive information about a child's activities and behaviour
■ A situation which is not pre-structured by the observer, and therefore has a good chance of providing accurate information without accidental bias
■ Good systems for recording language and communication skills
■ A structure for analysing the evidence in the observation.

Limitations of the 'Target Child's system:

■   It makes heavy demands on the observer, who has to be prepared to learn and practise the system

■   It requires the observer to be able to write quickly and to summarise accurately and without distortion.

Sample of a completed 'Target Child' observation sheet

CHILD'S INITIALS: AB   AGE: 3.5   DATE & TIME OBSERVED:

	ACTIVITY RECORD	LANGUAGE RECORD	TASK	SOCIAL
1.	TC at water tray, pouring water from one container to another and back, one container in each hand	C ▸ TC My Gran's coming	MAN	PAIR
2.	TC fills large jug with water and repeatedly pours it from a height into water tray, watching splashes		MAN	PAIR/P
3.	TC refills jug to pour again. C puts colander beneath TC's flow of water	TC ▸ C Don't. Oh, it goes out all the holes	MAN	PAIR
4.	A brings plastic bottles with holes pierced at different levels	A ▸ TC What do you think will happen if we pour water in here from your jug? TC ▸ A It will squirt out	MAN	PAIR
5.	A holds container with holes. TC carefully pours from jug. A hands over container with holes. C holds it while TC pours.	C ▸ A Let me do it.	MAN	PAIR
6.	C & TC pouring, taking turns	A ▸ TC & C Which holes does it come out of hardest? C ▸ A The bottom ones TC ▸ A Because it's fuller	EX	PAIR
7.	TC leaves water. Goes to block play area. Starts to arrange blocks in a row.		SSC	SOL
8.	Puts an extra block on top of the block at one end of the row and starts to push the row along from the other end.	TC (makes brm, brrmm noises) A ▸ TC Have you had any milk yet, AB? Do you want some?	PRE	SOL
9.	TC goes to snack table, takes her name card from one bowl and puts it in the other, takes cup of milk and sits down.	TC ▸ C I made a train C ▸ TC (about trains	DA	SG
10.	Drinks milk.	TC ▸ A Can I have a biscuit? A ▸ TC No biscuits today. Do you want a piece of apple? TC ▸ A Yes please TC ▸ C I like biscuits best.	DA	SG

Selective observations

Sometimes specific information is needed about a particular child. In this case, a general narrative observation might not be the most useful approach. Selective observations are designed to target a single aspect of a child's activity or behaviour.

Event sampling

Sometimes pre-school staff and parents want to understand why particular children behave the way they do. Event sampling is a way of trying to understand more about an event by recording what comes before it and what follows it.

Event sampling can be useful if a pre-school wants to establish the circumstances that support a particular kind of activity, for example, how complex co-operative play is encouraged.

In order to carry out an event sample observation, the observer identifies the particular type of event she/he is seeking to observe, for example, a child making unsuccessful attempts to join in other children's play. When the sought action or behaviour occurs, it is described as fully as possible in the middle of three columns. The first and last columns record what preceded the event and what followed it. The findings can indicate what causes the particular event which was being observed. For example, the observation may show that the child who makes unsuccessful attempts to join other children's play pushes herself into the children's activity without looking at or talking to them.

Antecedent	Event	Subsequent Events
Children A, B & C at water tray. Child D pushes in between children B and C and snatches water wheel.	Children A and B and C say they do not want D to play with them.	One adult goes to comfort the children at the water tray; another goes to talk to D.
Child E examines the boxes of sticking activity. Adult watches. Child F joins the activity and says to Child E and adult, "I went on a train like the one in the story. We went to a big station." Adult asks the children, if they would like to make a station. They say yes.	Children E and F use boxes and pieces of card to make a train station.	Ideas about the station come from child E and F, they use one another's ideas. Adult watches.

What an event sampling observation can offer:

- Provides information about a particular type of activity or behaviour and the context in which it takes place
- Can provide information about the causes of particular types of activity or behaviour.

Limitations of an event sampling observation:

- Can be time consuming if used for activities or behaviours that happen infrequently.

Spider's Web

This observation method is used to see if there are patterns in children's activity and behaviour. The observation indicates what activities the child uses and for how long, and how often a child returns to any base which is used. It traces the movement of the child from one activity to another and back to the 'safe base', recording the length of time the child spends at each activity and at the safe base.

The activities available are listed around the edge of a circle including the 'safe base'. The activity at which the child starts is ringed. The child's movements are indicated by arrowed lines, and numbers at the perimeter show how long the child has spent at each activity.

A new child may use her/his parent/carer or a particular activity, perhaps the dough table, as a 'safe base' from which to move out to take part in other activities.

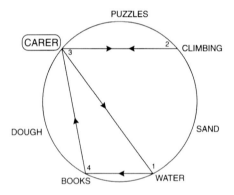

What a spider's web observation can offer:

- It can show the length of time the child is willing to be away from a point of security
- It can indicate the length of time the child can concentrate on a single activity
- It can show which activities are most attractive to that child. This might indicate something about the child's present range of interests or it might carry messages about the activities themselves. If, for example, one particular activity is consistently underused, the group might want to reconsider the way that activity is positioned or presented.

Limitations of the spider's web system of observation:

- It gives no indication of the quality of the child's experiences at the activities visited
- It does not show interactions with other adults or with other children.

Tracking

Sometimes it is useful to find out what activities a child experiences during the pre-school day/session. A child's keyworker may want information about the child's level of concentration at particular activities or to know whether a child is using the full range of activities provided by the setting. A tracking observation will show which activities a child uses and how long she/he spends at each. For this purpose, a rough plan of the group's layout is drawn and the child's movements are recorded by arrowed lines, with numbers to represent the length of time spent at each activity. It is often helpful to photocopy the layout plan for future use when carrying out tracking observations.

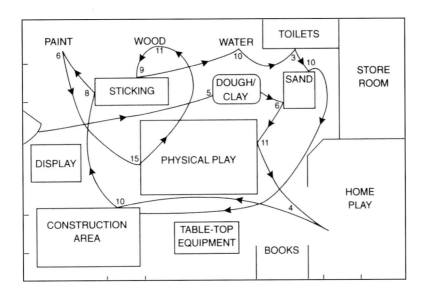

What a tracking system can offer:

■   information on what activities the child engages in

■   clues, from the child's choice of activities, about her/his current interests

■   hints from the child's choice of activities about what attracts the child to an activity. Are all the selected activities close to the door, for example, or directly supervised by an adult, or near a good source of natural light?

■   information on how long is spent at each activity; this can be used to assess a child's attention span.

Limitations of the tracking system:

■   there will be no information about what the child does at the various activities

■   the system does not record the child's social interactions.

Sociogram

This form of observation records contacts between people. It can be used to show how confident and successful children are in approaching and responding to adults and/or children, and whether they initiate or follow in social interactions. The 'approaches' indicated in the column headings include any sort of social contact, including opening a conversation, asking a question, making a suggestion, seeking or offering help or offering to join in. The response can be identified as positive or negative (P/N). Positive responses include smiling, responding to conversation, giving or accepting help and sharing equipment or activities. Negative responses include ignoring an approach, refusing help and moving equipment out of reach.

The completed example below suggests that the child under observation would like more exchanges with other children than he is getting. Negative responses to his approaches, however, discourage him from trying again for some time and/or make him turn to an adult.

There is a pro-forma for this kind of observation in the Appendix 3.

What a sociogram can offer:

- Accurate information on the number of social interactions
- An indication of whether the child mostly initiates or responds to interactions
- The type of response a child receives when initiating interactions
- The type of response the child makes to approaches from adults and other children.

Limitations of a sociogram:

- It cannot show the nature of interactions. When the child goes to the adult in the completed example below, for example, the diagram cannot show whether he is seeking comfort or practical help, or making a complaint.

SOCIOGRAM

CHILD'S NAME/INITIALS: Tariq S

DATE: 11 April 2001

OBSERVED BY: Daniel W

APPROACHES ADULT	RESP P/N	APPROACHES ADULT	RESP P/N	APPROACHES ADULT	RESP P/N	APPROACHES ADULT	RESP P/N
9.05	P						
		9.15	N				
						10.30	P
		10.40	P				
		10.45	P				
						11.10	P
		11.20	N				
11.25	P						
						11.55	P
		12.00	N				
12.05	P						

PARENT'S SIGNATURE

Curriculum-based observations

These are sometimes called assessment tasks. These are structured situations set up by the adults to establish whether a child has attained either a particular early learning goal or one of the stepping stones leading up to it.

If adults want to check, for example, that a child can "recognise numerals 1 to 9", they might jumble up the number dominoes, or any other set of numerals that can be arranged in random order, and invite the child to, "Show me a 6," or, "Can you find a 3?"

The child's attainments can be recorded straight into her/his record of achievement. Curriculum based observations are particularly useful for aspects of the early learning goals and stepping stones about which evidence is not likely to arise from children's self-chosen activities.

What curriculum-based observations can offer:

■ A clear indication of what a child can achieve in a particular situation
■ Information to build on in assessing the child's progress and creating an individual learning plan.

Limitations of curriculum-based observations:

■ There is a risk in trying to check the child's progress by looking at single skills in isolation. When questions are asked outside a context that is meaningful for the child, the results may not give a reliable picture of the child's understanding. The results of these tests, as in all other observations, need to be confirmed before they are used as a basis for action.

Observation grids

These seek very specific information in a context pre-selected by the observer. They usually operate on a 'snapshot' principle, recording very brief observations of a specific child/activity at stated intervals over a long period of time - a whole day or a week. They indicate only one aspect of the activity or of the child's behaviour. For example, if there is concern that some activities are being under-used in the setting, an activity grid might be completed to show just how frequently the various activities are being used.

Time sampling grid

Time sampling is an attempt to look at the play experience of a specific child by conducting a series of very brief observations at pre-set times simply to establish what the child is doing at those times. It can be a useful way of addressing concerns about a possible imbalance in the curriculum of an individual child. The observations are usually conducted at 10 to15 minute intervals throughout the day or session. The entry in the final column is ringed to indicate the presence of an adult.

Day/time	Location	Activity	Social context
Mon 9.15	Dough table	Making 'snakes'	Small group
9.30	Dough table	Making a road with cars on it	Pair
9.45	Snack table	Having milk and some apple	Small group, talking
10.00	Block corner	Building a tower	Solitary

What a time sample can offer:

■ Opportunity to build up a picture of the experiences the child encounters in the setting

■ Concise data, in a form easily shared with and understood by others

■ Evidence about whether a child is experiencing a balanced curriculum.

Limitations of a time sample:

■ There is no attempt to evaluate the quality of the child's experience

■ The observation cannot indicate reasons for the child's choice of activity.

Activity grid

A brief observation of the selected activity is usually conducted at 5 or 10 minute intervals for half an hour or more, and records the number of children at the activity, with a ring round the number if an adult is present.

Date	11.00	11.05	11.10	11.15	11.20	11.25	etc
Home play	3	4	6	7	7	2	
Books	1	1	5	6	6	2	
Clay	5	4	2	3	3	3	
Sticking	4	4	4	4	4	4	
Climbing frame	2	3	2	3	1	3	
etc							

What an activity grid can offer:

■ Accurate information about one aspect of the provision

■ Information quickly gathered and recorded: all the observer has to write for each observation is a number

■ Information leading to a reassessment of the activities themselves, the way they are presented, or the deployment of adult resources.

Limitations of the activity grid:

■ Nothing is shown about the quality of the children's experience at the activities, or their reasons for choosing them

■ The very narrow focus of the observation can prevent the observer from noticing other - perhaps more important - features that do not come within its scope

■ A completed activity grid cannot show what social groupings and/or interactions are taking place.

Assessment

CHAPTER 4 - ASSESSMENT

Once each half term Sascha's keyworker, Penny, goes through and analyses the evidence that has been placed in Sascha's record file since the last assessment of his progress. This analysis enables Penny to identify the progress Sascha has made in each area of learning and development.

The evidence placed in a child's record file provides information about the child's interests and what the child has said and done in the pre-school setting and at home. In order to make an assessment of the child's progress, the pre-school worker has to examine this evidence and make judgements about the stage that the child has reached in each area of learning and development. In order to make these judgements, pre-school workers will need to use their knowledge of child development and of the early learning goals for the Foundation Stage of children's education.

Examining the evidence

There is no one right way to examine the evidence collected in the children's record files. However, the chosen method needs to be systematic and thorough to ensure that all the evidence relevant to a particular area of learning and development has been identified. One approach to doing this is to take each of the Foundation Stage's six areas of learning and development in turn. Then, having reminded yourself of the early learning goals and stepping stones for the particular area of learning and development, to go through the evidence marking anything that is relevant to that area.

Once all the evidence, relevant to a particular area of learning and development has been identified, the pre-school worker needs to compare the evidence with the worker's knowledge about the stages through which children progress in that area. This comparison will enable the worker to make a judgement about the stage that the child has reached.

Making judgements

The early learning goals and the stepping stones for each area of learning and development provide a guide to the stages through which children can be expected to progress. Children's actual progress is often through smaller stages than those given by the stepping stones and early learning goals. For this reason, pre-school workers will find it useful to use their knowledge of child development to break down some of the stepping stones and early learning goals into these smaller stages. These can then be compared with the evidence about a particular child to make judgements about her/his progress. Appendix 4 provides an example of breaking down the early learning goals and stepping stones for each area of learning and development into smaller stages.

As the pre-school worker compares the evidence with the smaller stages in that area, she/he will make a judgement that the child has reached a particular stage if several pieces of evidence show the child to be behaving in ways typical of that stage.

For example, Sascha's key worker, Penny, might find that in the area of development of knowledge and understanding of the world, Sascha has:

■ a target child observation describing Sascha taking part in a floating and sinking activity and as each object is placed in the water saying either "It's swimming" or "It's on the bottom"

- an informal note saying that Sascha talked about seeing the leaves falling off the trees when he went to the park with his family
- a note about a conversation with Sascha's dad, who said that Sascha had drawn the rest of the family's attention to the leaves falling from the trees
- an informal note about Sascha rolling small cars down a hill made from wooden blocks and a long strip of plywood and saying whether each car stayed on or fell off the hill.

Penny's comparison of this evidence with the stages of progress for children's knowledge and understanding of the world will lead her to make the judgement that Sascha has reached the stage of:

'Comment on what is happening'

This is one of the smaller stages through which children progress to achievement of the early learning goal:

'Ask questions about why things happen and how things work'

Using assessments of children's progress

As the pre-school worker identifies the stages that a child has reached in each of the areas of learning and development, it will be important for the worker to make a written record of them. As Chapters 5 and 6 will show, written records of children's achievement make easier the tasks of sharing information about children's progress with their parents and planning with them for their children's further progress.

Records of Progress

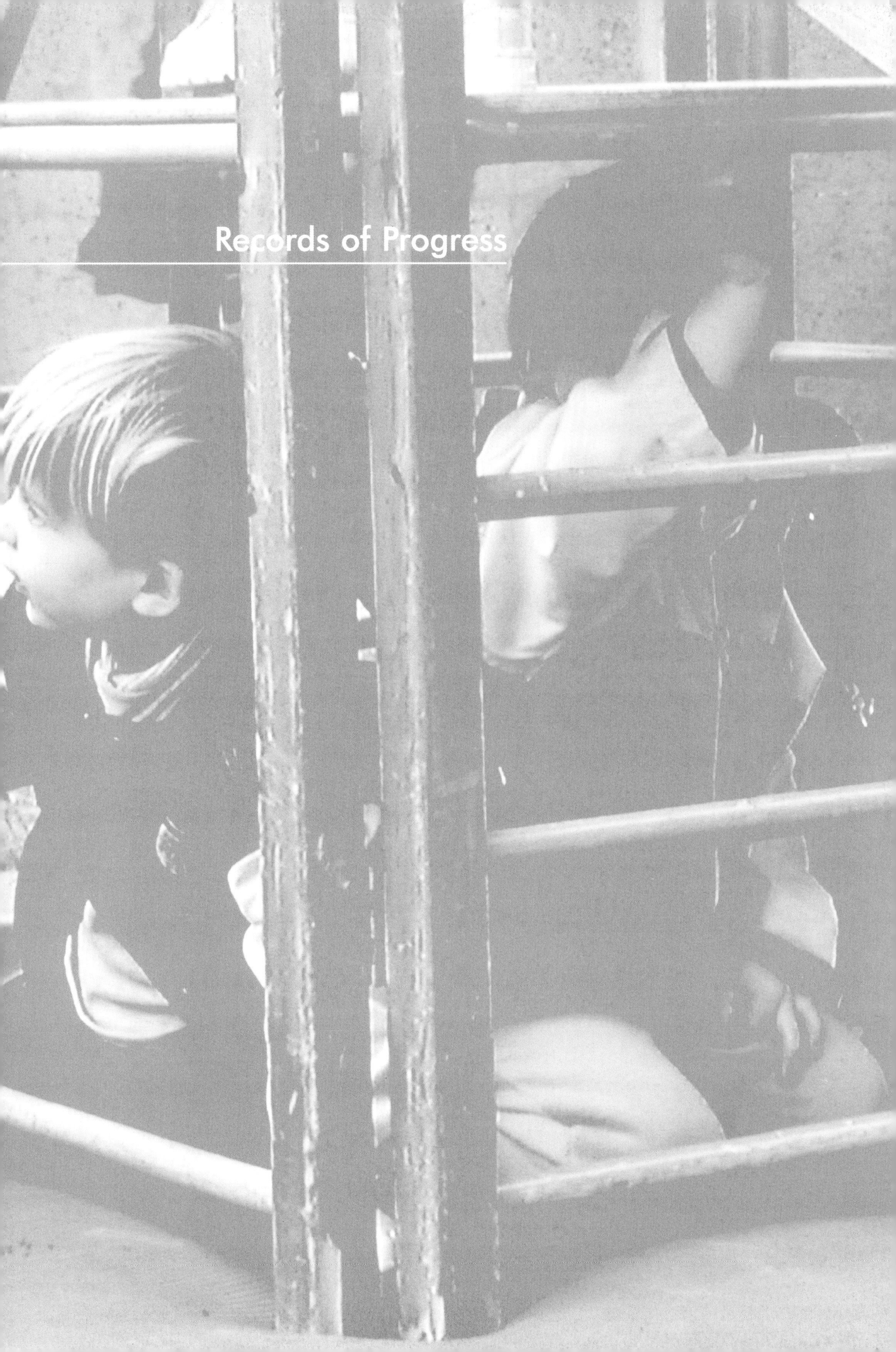

CHAPTER 5 - RECORDS OF PROGRESS

Maintaining a written record of individual children's achievements in each area of learning and development helps pre-school settings with:

- planning to further children's progress
- tracing children's rate of progress
- sharing children's stages of progress with parents
- evaluating the curriculum provided by the pre-school setting.

Planning to further children's progress

A written record provides a clear statement about what a particular child has achieved in each area of learning and development. This can be referred to when deciding what are appropriate targets to set to help to further the child's learning and development.

Tracing children's rate of progress

The written record provides something that can be compared with the expected targets for children's learning and enables the adult to check on a child's rate of progress. This will give the pre-school setting an indication of whether a particular child is likely to achieve the early learning goals by the end of the Foundation Stage. If it seems that a particular child is progressing at a rate that means that she/he is not likely to do so, the pre-school setting will want to consider whether the targets it is setting for her/him are appropriate and whether it is providing the right activities and support. Further investigation by the pre-school setting in partnership with the child's parents may show that she/he needs extra support.

Sharing children's stages of progress with parents

A written record provides something that a pre-school worker and a child's parents can look at together so that they talk about what the child has achieved and what they think they should be helping her/him to achieve next.

Evaluating the curriculum provided by the pre-school setting

The comparisons of each child's achievements with the expected targets for children's progress in each area of learning and development help the setting to see how effective its curriculum is in promoting the children's learning. If, on the whole, the children are progressing at a rate that means they will achieve the early learning goals in each area of learning and development by the end of the reception year, this indicates that the setting's curriculum is being effective. The comparison might, however, show that the children are not progressing at the expected rate in one or more specific areas of learning and development. If this is the case, the pre-school setting will need to examine the curriculum that is being provided for this or these areas and decide what changes should be made to make the provision more effective.

How to record

There is no single method for making written records of the assessments of the stages of children's progress. The method chosen by any particular pre-school setting should enable the records to fulfil the purposes that have just been described.

The pro-forma in Appendix 4 illustrates one method that can be used to record the stages of learning and development that children have achieved. This pro-forma sets out the early learning goals and the linked stepping stones for each area of learning and development.

Some of the stepping stones have been broken down into the smaller stages through which children's learning and development will progress. The date at which the child achieves the smaller stages and stepping stones is recorded on the form. Although the method involves the use of several pieces of paper for each child, it lays out the stages and steps through which children move to achievement of the early learning goals and helps with the task of tracing children's rate of progress.

An alternative method is to use the pro-forma in Appendix 5. In this method, the assessment of the stage/s of the child's progress in each area of learning and development is recorded. The date on which the assessment was made is also noted. This method makes it easy to see a child's achievements in each area of learning and development at a particular time. In order to identify the child's rate of progress in each area of learning and development, these achievements will need to be compared with the goals, stepping stones and smaller stages for each area.

The children's written records of achievement should be easily accessible to the people who need to see and use them: the children, their parents and the staff members whose responsibility it is to make the records. By sharing records of achievement with the children, parents and keyworkers can celebrate the achievements with the children and talk with them about what they might achieve next. Having access to the children's records of achievement will help parents and keyworkers to work together to decide on appropriate targets for progressing the children's development and to agree on appropriate actions to help the children to achieve these targets.

Storing records

Earlier chapters have referred to children's record files. Many pre-school settings use these to store children's records of achievement. They have a large box or folder for each child to store:

- the child's record of achievement
- evidence collected about the child
- the child's individual learning plan.

Keeping together all of the information about each child means that everything relevant to promoting the child's learning and development is in one place and provides an overall picture of the child's learning and development.

If pre-school settings decide to have this type of record file for each child, it will be important to store the files where they are easily available to everyone who needs access to them: pre-school staff, the child's parents and the child herself/himself.

All parents should have an equal opportunity to access the information in their child's record file. It will therefore be important for it to be stored in a way that enables them to access it. This will mean making the information available in parents' preferred written languages and ensuring access to written records is not the only means of sharing information about children's progress. In addition to supporting access to the record file, there should be opportunities for parents to talk with pre-school staff and, in particular, with their child's keyworker or the member of staff responsible for looking after their child's record file.

The case study about Nicky in Chapter 2 shows that it is a good idea for children to be able to access their record files to put examples of their work in them.

Giving children access to their record files in this way enables them to have a stake in them. Children are themselves eager to grow and develop. If, as was described earlier in this chapter, children's records of achievement and the targets for their progress are shared with them, children can be involved in deciding for themselves that a particular piece of their work should be added to the evidence in the file. For example, one of Smo's targets is `To write his own name from memory without help'. This target was shared with Smo and he came into his pre-school one morning saying, "I did my name all by myself on this card. I am putting it in my box."

Supporting the children's interest in what is in their record files serves several useful purposes:

- it supports the children's developing sense of their own autonomy.
- it prevents the record-keeping process from being seen - by children or parents - as a negative search for weaknesses rather than a positive celebration of strengths.
- it can counter any negative feelings children might already have about themselves.
- by helping them to see all the ways they are making progress, it can give them confidence that progress is possible, even in areas they find more difficult.

Children's record files and other professionals

Some children in the pre-school setting may be receiving help from other professionals. The information which the pre-school setting has about a child's progress could be helpful to the professional working with the child and her/his family. If all the information about the child's progress is kept in a record file, the shared information will provide an all round picture of the child's progress.

If a child's record file is shared with other professionals working with her/him, this will be something that the pre-school setting and the child's parents have agreed should happen.

Confidentiality

The record file for an individual child will contain a lot of information about that child. Parents must be confident that material gathered on their own child will be treated with respect. They have a right to see the records kept on their own children but they do not have a right to see other children's records. This means that:

- It is a good idea to encourage parents to sign the evidence, records of achievement and individual learning plans in their child's record file when they have seen them.
- Parents looking at their child's record file should not access other children's files. If the files are stored so that they are accessible for children to place evidence in them, the pre-school setting will need to have a policy which makes it clear that parents only have access to their own children's files and all parents must agree to abide by this policy.
- Individual records kept on a computer database should be password-protected.

Records about individual people may be used only for the purpose for which they were first created. If the records in the pre-school are created to assist with planning within the setting, they cannot be used for a different purpose, for example to help with transition to primary school, unless all those involved agree with the change.

The provisions of the Data Protection Act include data kept on computer file and those kept on paper. Parents have a right to see any information or record stored relating to their child.

Occasionally, detailed observation can bring to light sensitive information about a child, or might prompt parents to confide in the keyworker about matters regarding the child's family. In these circumstances, it is essential to establish with the parents how widely they are willing for the information to be shared. The group must be able to work closely with parents for the sake of the child, and to this end parents must be confident that sensitive information will go no further than they wish.

Rarely, observations on a child might lead to concern about the child's well-being and safety, and possibly to suspicions of abuse. Observations of this sort will be kept quite separate. It can be useful to set up a repeat observation, preferably conducted by another member of staff or on a paired basis, to try to eliminate any subjective element in the original observation. All settings should have a special system for recording confidential material of this sort,[2] and such suspicions should be dealt with in line with the setting's Child Protection policy and the requirements of the Area Child Protection Committee.

[2] See Pre-school Learning Alliance publication, "Confidential Incident Record".

Plans

CHAPTER 6 - PLANS

Rebecca's record of achievement shows that in her mathematical development she has reached the stage of reciting the numbers 1 to 9 in the correct order. Rebecca's parents and her keyworker have noticed that she shows an interest in counting the objects, which she uses in her play. Rebecca says she likes knowing how many there are of the things she is using. During their discussions about her record of achievement Rebecca's keyworker and parents agree that the next target for her mathematical development should be to count reliably 5 objects, relating the number names to the objects on a one-to-one basis. The keyworker suggests that providing Rebecca with opportunities to take part in activities, which use one-to-one correspondence, will help her to achieve the target. Rebecca's keyworker and parents decide to help her to achieve her target by building on her interest in books. They will share number and counting books with her and respond to her attempts at counting by helping her to touch each object as she says the correct number name. They decide to make sure that puzzles that involve matching objects one for one are available for Rebecca.

The target for Rebecca's mathematical development and the activities to support her achievement of it will form part of her individual learning plan. A record of achievement shows the stages that a child has reached in her/his learning and development. An individual learning plan shows how a child will be helped to move forward to the next stages.

The purpose of the individual learning plan

All children need an individual learning plan, in order to ensure that their existing achievements and interests are built on and developed. A child's individual learning plan does this by setting appropriate targets for her/him in each area of learning and development, and by identifying strategies to help the child to achieve these targets. Having an individual learning plan for each child ensures that thought and care has been given to what the pre-school setting needs to do to progress each child's learning and development. Many pre-school settings update children's individual learning plans each half term.

Creating the individual learning plan

Before creating individual learning plans for the children, keyworkers and other staff will have already:

■ Collected evidence about each child's interests, activities and behaviours
■ Analysed the evidence to assess each child's current stages of learning and development
■ Made a written record of each child's progress.

Creating the individual learning plans will involve pre-school staff in identifying appropriate next steps to help the children to progress from their current stage in each area of the children's learning and development.

Setting targets
In order to set targets for children's learning and development, pre-school staff will draw on their knowledge of:

■ the norms of child development
■ the requirements of the early learning goals, and of the 'stepping stones' that lead towards them.

Chapter 5 explained why, when using the early learning goals and their linked stepping stones, from QCA's 'Curriculum guidance for the Foundation Stage', it can be useful to break down some of the stepping stones into smaller steps. As well as being useful for assessing the stage of children's progress, the smaller steps, listed in Appendix 4 can also be used to set appropriate targets for children's learning and development.

The case study about Rebecca provides an example of the processes that pre-school staff will need to use to set targets for children's learning and development.

The target set for Rebecca's mathematical development was intended to move her forward through an achievable step from her present level of achievement. Rebecca had reached the stage of knowing the correct order of the numbers 1 to 9 and showed an interest in finding out how many. Counting up to 5 objects by using the correct number name as each object is counted would be a step that Rebecca would be likely to be able to make and makes it an appropriate target to set for her mathematical development.

The next task in creating Rebecca's individual learning plan was to decide what should be done to help her to achieve the target of 'counting up to 5 objects by using the correct number name as each object is counted.'

Identifying appropriate strategies
The strategies for helping the child to achieve the identified targets for her/his learning and development include activities that will be provided in the pre-school setting and at home, and the adult support that it might be useful to give to the child as s/he takes part in the identified activities. In deciding with a child's parents what these activities should be, pre-school staff will use their knowledge of child development to identify which particular play activities might be used at pre-school and at home to promote specific aspects of the child's learning and development.

In the case study, Rebecca's keyworker used her knowledge of children's mathematical development to suggest that activities giving Rebecca experiences of one to one matching would help her to count objects using one number name for one object.

A further consideration in choosing appropriate activities will be the child's existing interests, Rebecca's interest in books led to the decision to share number and counting books with her.

Rebecca's plan identified that adults would support her attempts at counting by helping her to touch each object as she counted if off.

As the activities identified in children's individual learning plans, are implemented the cycle of evidence collection, assessment, record keeping and planning will begin again. In Rebecca's case, her keyworker and her parents will be collecting evidence about her counting activities. Then, these will be analysed to see if they show that Rebecca can accurately count up to 5 objects using one number name for each object, consistently.

Planning as a shared activity

When pre-school staff share with children's parents the task of planning to progress individual children's learning and development, parents will be able to use opportunities that arise as part of children's life at home to help them to achieve the targets for their learning and development.

In Rebecca's case, her and her brother's interest in playing with his new magnetic fishing game could be used to help Rebecca to count accurately the fish she catches.

Even very young children can be powerful agents in their own learning. Talking with them about the targets and in their plans, can help in many ways:

■ Children learn more readily when they are actively involved in their own learning

■ Children have a right to know what direction they are going in, and what is being attempted on their behalf

■ Children who understand what staff are trying to achieve, and the thinking behind the strategies they are using, are in a position to add their active co-operation, for example, a child who knows that writing her first name without any adult help is one of her targets may ask to place her successful attempt at doing this in her record file

■ Knowing what the target was enables children to share in the satisfaction of succeeding.

Priorities

Children's individual learning plans should help them to make progress in all areas of learning and development. As part of setting targets for each area and identifying appropriate strategies to help children to achieve them, it will be important to remember the effect that children's progress in one area may have upon their progress in other areas.

A child's ability to hold and manipulate objects in a pincer grip will affect their development in several other areas:

■ A child's ability to gain pleasure and confidence in looking at books is affected by her/his ability to turn over the pages of books one by one

■ A pincer grip gives a child more control over pencils, paint brushes and glue brushes. This control can increase a child's ability to be creative

■ Having good control of her/his pencil will help a child who has grasped the idea of using written language to communicate to form the letters she/he wishes to write

■ A child's ability to develop personal independence will be helped, if s/he can manipulate the fasteners on clothing and handle cutlery well enough to be independent in dressing and in dealing with a range of foods.

Sometimes a child's keyworker and parents may decide that her/his progress with a particular skill, such as using a pincer grip, is holding up her/his progress in other areas. If this is the case, they will probably decide to concentrate on helping the child to make progress with the particular skill.

Strategies for helping a child to hold and manipulate objects using a pincer grip could include:

■ activities that involve picking up and sprinkling powder-like materials, for example, sticking activities using glitter and feeding the goldfish

■ using pegboards and threading activities, starting with very large pegs and beads

■ encouraging the child to twist and squeeze pieces of dough, either in exploratory play or in cooking.

The layout of an individual learning plan

There is no single correct way to set out a child's learning plan and each setting will want to find the presentation that best suits their own needs, and the needs of the children and families at present attending. However, each should contain the following information:

- Child's name
- Child's age
- Name of keyworker (or other responsible member of staff)
- Date of the plan
- The target(s) for the child in each area of learning and development
- The strategies to be used to help the child reach the targets (including activities, equipment and adult input)
- The date at which progress will be reviewed.

The completed plan that follows on page 46 offers one suggested layout, and there is a pro-forma, which can be photocopied, for this method in the Appendix 6.

Using individual learning plans to create session plans and medium term plans

The setting's medium-term plan will be created to cover specific aspects of the long-term plan for the group as a whole,[3] and the session plan will look at ways to implement parts of the medium-term plan. However, as children's individual learning plans are reviewed, fresh learning targets will be created for the children. These targets will need to inform session and medium-term planning for the group as a whole, and keyworkers will take responsibility for ensuring that this happens. Most session plans have a special column for highlighting the learning needs of specific children.

It is possible to integrate individual learning plans into the broader plans for the group as a whole, because there will be common themes in the targets that have been set for individual children and because most activities provided in pre-school settings can be managed in ways that allow them to support more than one area of learning and development. When pre-school staff look at the individual learning plans of the children in the setting, they will probably find that several children have similar targets. For example, the staff in Rebecca's pre-school will probably find that several children have counting groups of objects using the correct number name for each object as a target. In which case, the medium term plan for the setting will include work on 'numbers as labels and for counting' and the session plans for implementing the medium term plan will include a number of activities that provide opportunities for counting. These could be board games, counting rhymes with opportunities for counting the objects in the rhyme and playing hopscotch. When they are creating session plans, pre-school staff will find that each activity can be used to meet a number of children's individual learning targets:

- George, whose target is to take turns
- Rebecca, who is working on counting objects through using the correct number name as each object is counted
- Omobola, who has as a target to manipulate objects using a thumb and finger pincer grip.

A board game with a dice and counters played by a small group of children and an adult could be used to support George, Rebecca and Omobola's targets.

[3] See Pre-school Learning Alliance publication on the pre-school curriculum.

44

As the pre-school setting implements its medium term plans, session plans and plans for individual children's learning, staff, parents and children will look for and collect evidence of children's achievement of their targets. So another cycle of evidence collection, assessment, record keeping, planning and implementation will begin. Like all such cycles its intention will be to progress the learning and development of each child in the pre-school setting.

INDIVIDUAL LEARNING PLAN

CHILD'S NAME: Lisa J   CHILD'S AGE: 2.10

NAME OF KEYWORKER   Lesley

DATE OF PLAN: 30 .10.01   DATE FOR REVIEW: 10.12.01

TARGET	STRATEGIES TO BE USED		DATE	COMMENTS
Creative development Use musical instruments to respond to and play out stories	■	Build on Lisa's enjoyment of being read to by reading stories that include musical instruments and that focus on sounds, and by talking about what it would be like to make the sounds in the stories.		
	■	Have instruments in the music corner that are capable of reproducing the sounds in the stories.		
Communication, language and literacy Repeat the final sound of familiar words and find other words that end with the same sound	■	Read rhyme books with Lisa and talk with her about the sounds used to make the rhyme in them.		
	■	Involve Lisa in making and using a card game in which cards with objects whose name ends with the same sound are matched.		
Personal, social and emotional development With adult encouragement asks others for ideas and help with tasks, and suggests ways of doing tasks	■	Encourage Lisa to take part in small group activities that set the children a challenge and require them to help one another - water play and siphoning; construction with wooden blocks.		

PARENT'S SIGNATURE

DATE

APPENDIX

Appendix 1 - UNPLANNED OBSERVATION

Date

Name of observer

Background to observation

Name of child

OBSERVATION

PARENT'S SIGNATURE

DATE

Appendix 2 - TARGET CHILD OBSERVATION SHEET

CHILDS NAME/INITIALS: SEX: AGE:

DATE & TIME OBSERVED:

	ACTIVITY RECORD	LANGUAGE RECORD	TASK	SOCIAL
1				
2				
3				
4				
5				
6				
7				
8				
9				
10				

PARENT'S SIGNATURE

DATE

Appendix 3 - PRO-FORMA FOR SOCIOGRAM

CHILD'S NAME/INITIALS:

DATE:

OBSERVED BY:

APPROACHES ADULT	RESP P/N	APPROACHES CHILD	RESP P/N	APPROACHED BY ADULT	RESP P/N	APPROACHED BY CHILD	RESP P/N

PARENT'S SIGNATURE

DATE

Appendix 4 - PROGRESS TOWARDS THE EARLY LEARNING GOALS

NAME OF CHILD:

DATE OF BIRTH:

Personal, social and emotional development

STEPPING STONE	SMALLER STAGES IN PROGRESS	DATE ACHIEVED
Shows curiosity	▪ Is Interested in what is shown to her/him ▪ Wants to find out things for self	
Has a strong exploratory impulse	▪ Explores thoroughly what is happening in some activities ▪ Explores thoroughly what is happening in all activities	
Takes risks and explores within the environment		
EARLY LEARNING GOAL **Continues to be interested, excited and motivated to learn**		
Has a positive approach to new experiences	▪ With adult encouragement takes part in activities newly introduced to the setting ▪ On own initiative takes part in some activities newly introduced to the setting	
Shows increasing independence in selecting and carrying out activities	▪ Shows willingness to take part in increasingly difficult tasks ▪ Tries out new ways of using the equipment and materials available with the activities	

Shows confidence in linking up with others for support and guidance	■ With adult encouragement, asks others for ideas and help with tasks, and suggests ways for doing tasks ■ On own initiative asks others for ideas and help with tasks, and suggests ways for doing tasks
EARLY LEARNING GOAL **Is confident to try new activities, initiate ideas and speak in a familiar group**	
Displays high levels of involvement in activities	■ On some occasions listens to what others are saying ■ With adult encouragement carries tasks through to completion, including self-initiated tasks ■ On own initiative carries some tasks to completion including self-initiated tasks ■ With adult encouragement, sits quietly when this is appropriate ■ Spends an increasing period of time occupied in an increasing range of tasks, including self-initiated tasks ■ On own initiative carries most tasks through to completion including self-initiated tasks ■ On most occasions recognises for self when it is appropriate to sit quietly
EARLY LEARNING GOAL **Maintains attention, concentrates and sits quietly when appropriate**	
Separates from main carer with support	

Separates from main carer with confidence

Talks freely about her/his home and community
- Describes significant events from home
- Describes significant experiences that have taken place in the setting
- Shows feelings in the way she/he participates in activities in the setting
- Uses words to label the feelings associated with events from home
- Uses words to label the feelings associated with events in the setting
- Makes links between events in the setting and significant events at home
- Make links between current and previous events in the early years setting

Responds to significant experiences, showing a range of feelings when appropriate

Shows care and concern for self
- With encouragement takes steps to make own needs, views and feelings known
- Takes steps to make own needs, views and feelings known

Expresses needs and feelings in appropriate ways
- States own needs, views and feelings
- Describes own needs, views and feelings

Initiates interactions with others
- With encouragement listens to the needs, views and feelings of others
- Listens to the needs, views and feelings of others

EARLY LEARNING GOAL

Has a developing awareness of her/his own needs, views and feelings and is sensitive to the needs, views and feelings of others

- Notices other people's expression of their needs, views and feelings
- Responds appropriately to the needs, views and feelings of others

Has a sense of belonging

- Takes part in cultural events related to own culture in the early years setting
- Talks about cultural events that are part of home life

Has a sense of self as a member of different communities

- Makes links between events related to own culture at home and in the early years setting
- Takes part in cultural events that belong to cultures other than her/his own in the early years setting
- Talks about cultural events that are part of cultures other than her/his own
- Makes positive links between events in her/his own culture and the cultures of others

EARLY LEARNING GOAL

Has a developing respect for her/his own culture and beliefs and those of other people

Feels safe and secure and demonstrates a sense of trust

- Responds to initiatives from others to join activities or conversations

Seeks out others to share experiences

- Tries to join in with other people's activities
- Invites others to join in her/his activities
- Starts conversations with others

Relates and makes attachments to members of the pre-school

- Joins in activities and conversations with some adults and children
- Joins in activities and conversations with most adults and children in the pre-school

Forms good relationships with adults and peers

Demonstrates flexibility and adapts this behaviour to difficult events, social situations and changes in routine

- Needs adult prompting and support to take turns, share and work with others within the rules of the early years setting
- Starts to take turns, share and work with others
- Shows some awareness of the rules of the setting

Values and contributes to her/his well-being and self-control

- On most occasions takes turns, shares and works with others
- Shows awareness of the rules of the setting
- Takes turns, shares and works with others, on own initiative, within the rules of the early years setting

EARLY LEARNING GOAL

EARLY LEARNING GOAL

Works as part of a group or class, taking turns and sharing fairly, understanding that there need to be agreed values and codes of behaviour for groups of people, including adults and children to work together harmoniously

Begins to accept the needs of others with support	■ With adult guidance recognises and sees that behaviour is acceptable or unacceptable because of the effect it has on others ■ Responds positively to adult guidance on acceptable and unacceptable behaviour
Shows care and concern for others, for living things and the environment	■ Knows that some behaviour is acceptable and some is not because of its effect on other people, living things and the environment ■ On some occasions behaves in acceptable ways towards others, living things and the environment
Has an awareness of the boundaries set and behavioural expectations within the setting	■ On most occasions behaves in acceptable ways towards others, living things and the environment ■ Gives reasons why particular types of behaviour are acceptable and unacceptable

EARLY LEARNING GOAL

Understands what is right and wrong and why

Begins to accept the needs of others, with support	■ With adult help recognises the consequences of own words and actions ■ Takes adult suggested steps to deal with the consequences of own words and actions
Shows confidence and ability to stand up for own rights	■ With adult help decides how to take the steps to deal with the consequences of own words and actions ■ Makes own suggestions about how to deal with the consequences of her/his words and actions
Considers the consequences of her/his words and actions for herself/himself and others	
Shows willingness to tackle problems and enjoys self-chosen challenges	■ With adult prompting and help copes with clothes without fasteners ■ Can carry out personal hygiene tasks with prompting and help from adult ■ With adult prompting copes with clothes without fasteners ■ Can carry out personal hygiene tasks independently with prompting from adult ■ Can cope with clothes without fasteners ■ With adult help copes with clothes with fasteners

EARLY LEARNING GOAL

Operates independently within the environment and shows confidence in linking up with others for support and guidance

- Copes independently with some clothes fastenings, asking for help with more difficult ones
- Can carry out personal hygiene tasks without adult prompting or help
- Can cope with clothes with increasingly difficult fasteners

Dresses and undresses independently and manages own personal hygiene

Demonstrates a sense of pride in own achievement

- On occasions when chooses and uses activities shows pleasure in the results
- Shares pleasure in the results of activities with others

Takes initiative and manages developmentally appropriate tasks

- With adult help takes part in tasks that extend what is known and what can do
- Chooses for self tasks that extend what is known and can do
- Recognises and takes up opportunities that arise to develop a task in which engaged

Operates independently within the environment and shows confidence in linking up with others for support and guidance

- Takes part in an increasing number of tasks that extend what is known and can do
- When problems arise with tasks and help is offered, makes suggestions about the form it might take
- When problems arise with tasks, explains to others the help that is required

Selects and uses activities and resources independently

Makes connections between parts of her/his life experience

- Demonstrates or talks about experiences at home
- Make links between experiences at home and experiences in the pre-school setting

Shows a strong sense of self as a member of different communities such as her/his family or setting

- Shows an increasing awareness of the links between experiences in the pre-school and experiences at home
- Shows interest in other children's accounts of activities which are part of their home life

Has an awareness of, and shows interest and enjoyment in, cultural and religious differences

- With encouragement takes part in a range of cultural and religious events
- Takes part in a range of cultural and religious events
- Notices similarities between the events belonging to different cultures and religions
- Notices and comments positively on the differences in the various cultural and religious events

Understands that people have different needs, views, cultures and beliefs, that need to be treated with respect

Has a strong sense of self as a member of different communities such as her/his family and setting	■ With adult prompting shares experiences from home with others in the setting ■ With adult prompting shares her/his needs and ideas with others ■ Takes the initiative in sharing experiences from home with others in the setting ■ Takes the initiative in sharing needs and ideas with some adults and other children in the setting	
Has a positive self-image and shows that she/he is comfortable with herself/himself	■ Takes the initiative in sharing her/his experiences, needs and ideas with an increasing range of adults and children in the setting ■ Shows pride in the activities and ideas that are part of her/his cultural background ■ Offers her/his ideas and abilities as a means of moving forwards group tasks	

EARLY LEARNING GOAL

Understands that she/he can expect others to treat her/his needs, views, culture and beliefs with respect

Communication, language and literacy

STEPPING STONES	SMALLER STAGES IN PROGRESS	DATE ACHIEVED
Uses words and/or gestures, including body language such as eye contact and facial expressions to communicate	■ Uses these ways to communicate requests ■ Uses these ways to communicate information about what she/he is doing	

Uses simple statements and questions often linked to gestures

Uses information, rhythm and phrasing to make her/his meaning clear to others

Has emerging self-confidence to speak to others about wants and interests

Uses simple grammatical structures

Asks simple questions, often in the form of "where" or "when"

Talks alongside others, rather than with them. Uses talk to gain attention and initiate exchanges. Uses action rather than talk to demonstrate or explain to others

Initiates conversation, attends to and takes account of what others say, and uses talk to resolve disagreements

- Describes to others what she/he is doing
- Listens to others' descriptions of what she/he is doing
- Lets others finish before giving own ideas
- While engaging in activities, talks over and decides with other children and adults what they are going to do

Interacts with others, negotiating plans and activities and taking turns in conversation

Responds to simple instructions

Questions why things happen and gives explanations	■ Talks about what she/he is doing while playing ■ Listens to others talking about what is happening during play ■ Looks at and pretends to read books as part of play ■ Makes attempts to produce writing as part of play
Enjoys listening to and using spoken and written language, and readily turns to it in her/his play and learning	

EARLY LEARNING GOAL

Listens to others in one-to-one/small groups when conversation interests her/him	
Initiates a conversation, negotiates positions, pays attention to and takes account of others' views.	■ Makes comments to others and shows that expects response ■ Listens to increasing amounts of and increasingly complex talk ■ Responds appropriately to an increasing quantity and complexity of talk
Sustains attentive listening, responding to what she/he has heard by relevant comments, questions or actions	

EARLY LEARNING GOAL

Listens to favourite nursery rhymes, stories and songs. Joins in with repeated refrains, anticipating key events and important phrases	■ Enjoys rhymes, stories and songs on a one-to-one basis ■ Asks to listen to rhymes, stories and songs on a one-to-one basis ■ With encouragement joins group story, rhyme and song activities ■ Joins willingly in group story, rhyme and song activities ■ Joins in singing/saying/responding to songs, music, rhymes and poems
Listens to stories with increasing attention and recall	■ Asks questions about the stories being read/told ■ Immediately after a story has been read, talks about characters and events in a story ■ Remembers and repeats an increasing number of songs, rhymes and poems
Describes main story settings, events and principal characters	■ Talks about characters and events from an increasing number of stories ■ Retells stories which has heard ■ Makes up stories, songs, music, rhymes and poems during play
Listens with enjoyment and responds to stories, songs and other music, rhymes and poems and makes her/his own stories, songs, rhymes and poems	
Uses familiar words, often in isolation to identify what she/he does and does not want	

EARLY LEARNING GOAL

Uses vocabulary focused on objects and people who are of particular importance to her/him	
Builds up vocabulary that reflects the breadth of her/his experience	■ Shows interest in new words that name or describe what has seen and heard ■ Brings new words has learned into conversation
Begins to experiment with language describing possession	■ Uses the name of person to whom something belongs to indicate possession ■ Begins to use pronoun to indicate possession
Extends vocabulary, especially by grouping and naming	■ Shows an increasing interest in the proper name for newly encountered objects ■ Remembers correct names for newly encountered objects ■ Repeats words, showing an interest in their sounds
Uses vocabulary and forms of speech that are increasingly influenced by experience of books	■ Uses new words encountered in books ■ Uses correct forms of irregular past tenses ■ Thinks of real or made-up words that sound similar to words whose sound interests them

Extends her/his vocabulary, exploring the meanings and sounds of new words

Uses isolated words and phrases and/or gestures to communicate with those well known to her/him

EARLY LEARNING GOAL

Begins to use more complex sentences	
Uses a widening range of words to express or elaborate ideas	■ With prompting uses conventions for greeting people, making requests from them and accepting things from them ■ Remembers to use conventions for greeting people, making requests of them and accepting things from them
Links statements and sticks to a main theme or intention	
Consistently develops a simple story, explanation or line of questioning	
Uses language for an increasing range of purposes	■ To explain what has done ■ To explain what going to do ■ To explain why things happen ■ To explain what likes and dislikes
Confidently talks to people other than those who are well known to her/him	
Speaks clearly and audibly with confidence and control and shows awareness of the listener, for example by her/his use of conventions such as greetings, 'please' and 'thank you'	
Uses talk to give new meanings to objects and actions, treating them as symbols for other things	■ Gives new names to objects and actions in treating them as symbols for other things ■ Describes what newly named objects are doing in treating them as symbols or other things

EARLY LEARNING GOAL

Uses talk, actions and objects to recall and relive past experiences	■ Uses disjointed words and phrases as part of reliving past experiences ■ Links phrases into short accounts as part of reliving past experiences ■ In play, tells story of past experiences
Begins to use talk to pretend imaginary situations	■ Uses action and some talk to act out imaginary situations ■ Uses talk supported by some action to act out imaginary situations
Uses language to imagine and recreate roles and experiences	
Uses action, sometimes with limited talk, that is largely concerned with the 'here and now'	
Talks activities through reflecting on and modifying what she/he is doing	
Uses talk to connect ideas, explain what is happening and anticipate what might happen next	■ Describes what is happening ■ Links what is happening now to what happened before ■ Explains why think what is happening is happening ■ Uses descriptions of what is happening to explain what think might happen next
Begins to use talk instead of action to rehearse, re-order and reflect on past experiences, linking significant events from experience and from stories, paying attention to sequence and how events lead into one another	■ Uses a mixture of talk and action to do this ■ Uses decreasing amounts of action

EARLY LEARNING GOAL

Begins to make patterns in her/his experience through linking cause and effect, sequencing, ordering and grouping

- Uses talk to explain what will happen and why
- Uses talk to go through the order in which events happened
- Uses talk to go through the order in which things will happen
- Talks about events and objects that belong together explaining why

EARLY LEARNING GOAL

Uses talk to organise, sequence and clarify thinking, ideas, feelings and events

Enjoys rhyming activities

Shows awareness of rhyme and alliteration

- Recognises the initial sound of her/his own name
- Recognises other words beginning with the initial sound of his/her name
- Repeats the final sound of words in rhymes and familiar words

Continues a rhyming string

- Repeats the initial sound of familiar words and finds other words that begin with the same sound
- Repeats the final sound of familiar words and finds other words that end with the same sound

EARLY LEARNING GOAL

Hears and says initial and final sounds in words, and short vowel sounds within words

- Repeats the short vowel sounds within familiar words
- Finds words that contain the same short vowel sounds

Distinguishes one sound from another

Recognises rhythm in spoken words	■ Taps out the rhythm of own name ■ Taps out the rhythm of familiar words
Hears and says the initial sound in words and knows which letters represent some of the sounds	■ Recognises the symbol and sound of the first letter of her/his own name ■ Recognises the symbol and sound of the first letter of familiar words ■ Recognises the symbols and sounds of letters, using prompts from pictures of words beginning with the letter ■ Recognises without prompts the symbols and sounds of letters
EARLY LEARNING GOAL **Links sounds to letters, naming and sounding the letters of the alphabet**	
Distinguishes one sound from another	
Recognises rhythm in spoken words	■ Taps out the rhythm of own name ■ Taps out the rhythm of familiar words
EARLY LEARNING GOAL **Uses her/his phonic knowledge to write simple regular words and make phonetically plausible attempts at more complex words**	■ In talking about words, shows an awareness of the sounds which make them up ■ Attempts to use own knowledge of the sounds of words in order to write simple familiar words ■ Uses own knowledge of the sounds of words to try to write more complex words
Listens to and joins in with stories and poems, one-to-one and also in small groups	

Has favourite books

Understands the concept of a word

- Shows interest in repeated sounds/words in stories
- Joins in repeated sounds/words in stories
- Talks about particular words whose sounds interests her/him

Enjoys an increasing range of books

- Shows awareness of the text in books when being read to
- Comments on the text in books when being read to

EARLY LEARNING GOAL

Explores and experiments with sounds, words and texts

Begins to be aware of the way stories are structured

Suggests how the story might end

- Discusses the events of stories with the reader

EARLY LEARNING GOAL

Retells narratives in the correct sequence, drawing on the language patterns of stories

- Joins in other children's re-telling of familiar stories
- Acts out the events of familiar stories
- Retells to others the events of a story
- Uses phrases that structure stories, such as, 'Once upon a time'

Show an interest in illustrations and print in books and print in the environment

Begin to recognise some familiar words	■ Recognises the written form of his/her own name ■ Recognises familiar words in the environment ■ Recognises familiar words when looking at books
Reads a range of familiar and common words and simple sentences independently EARLY LEARNING GOAL	■ Recognises familiar and common words easily ■ Reads simple sentences with help ■ Reads simple sentences without help
Shows an interest in illustrations and print in books and print in the environment	
Knows that information can be relayed in the form of print	
Holds books the correct way up and turns pages	
Know that information can be retrieved from books and computers	■ Responds positively to adults' suggestions to look up information in books and computers ■ Suggests seeking information in books and computers and asks for adult help to do so
Knows that print carries meaning and, in English, is read from left to right and top to bottom EARLY LEARNING GOAL	■ Follows the adult's tracing of text while being read to ■ Traces a finger over the text in pretend reading ■ Talks about where the text on a page of a book starts and ends

Begins to be aware of the way stories are structured	
Suggests how a story might end	■ Responds to adults' comments and questions about the events in stories
Knows information can be relayed in the form of print	
Knows that information can be retrieved from books and computers	■ Responds positively to adults' suggestions to look up information in books and computers
	■ Suggests seeking information in books and computers and asks for adult help to do so
Shows an understanding of the elements of stories, such as main character, sequence of events and openings, and how information can be found in non-fiction texts to answer questions about where, who, why and how	■ Refers to elements in stories when being read to
	■ Uses appropriate elements of stories when re-telling them
Draws and paints sometimes giving meaning to work	
Ascribes meaning to work	
Begins to break the flow of speech into words	■ Asks adults to record her/his lists/instructions/descriptions of her/his work/ideas for a story
	■ With adult help adjusts speed of talking to help adult to record

EARLY LEARNING GOAL

Uses writing as a means of recording and communicating	■ Attempts to write lists/instructions as part of play ■ Attempts to copy adults' writing ■ Copies adults' writing accurately
EARLY LEARNING GOAL **Attempts writing for various purposes, using features of different forms such as lists, stories, instructions**	
Draws and paints sometimes giving meaning to work	
Ascribes meaning to work	
Uses writing as a means to recording and communicating	■ Copies own name ■ Writes own name from memory ■ Copies familiar words ■ Writes familiar words without copying ■ Copies sentences
EARLY LEARNING GOAL **Writes her/his own names and other things such as labels and captions and begins to form simple sentences, sometimes using punctuation**	■ Notices and includes capital letters and full stops when copying sentences ■ Includes capital letters and full stops in own writing
Engages in activities requiring hand-eye co-ordination	
Uses one-handed tools and equipment	
Draws lines and circles using gross motor movement	

Manipulates objects with increasing control	■ Picks up an increasing range of objects with a pincer grip ■ Manipulates objects using a pincer grip ■ Holds a pencil using a pincer grip
Begins to use anti-clockwise movement and retraces vertical lines	
Begins to form recognisable letters	■ Uses a pencil to copy recognisable letters ■ Uses a pencil to write recognisable letters
EARLY LEARNING GOAL **Uses a pencil and holds it effectively to form recognisable letters, most of which are correctly formed**	■ Copies letters so that they are correctly formed, beginning and ending them in the right place ■ Writes correctly formed letters, beginning and ending them in the right place

Mathematical development

STEPPING STONES	SMALLER STAGES IN PROGRESS	DATE ACHIEVED
Shows an interest in numbers and counting		
Uses some number names and number language spontaneously		
Enjoys joining in with number rhymes and songs		
Shows curiosity about numbers by offering comments or asking questions		

		EARLY LEARNING GOAL
Uses some number names accurately in play		
Shows confidence with numbers by initiating or requesting number activities	■	Can say the number names in order as part of a rhyme or song
Says and uses number names in order in familiar contexts	■	Can say the number names in order
Shows an interest in numbers and counting		
Enjoys joining in with number rhymes and songs		
Willingly attempts to count, with some numbers in the correct order		
Counts up to three or four objects by saying one number name for each item		
Counts up to six objects from a larger group	■	Points to objects one by one, using a number name for each object and using the number names in the right order, in order to count them for objects up to 9 objects
	■	Knows that the last number used when counting a group of objects tells us how many objects are there
Counts actions or objects that cannot be moved		
Counts an irregular arrangement of up to 10 objects		
Begins to count beyond 10		

EARLY LEARNING GOAL					
Counts reliably up to 10 everyday objects					
Recognises some numerals of personal significance					
Recognises numerals 1 to 5, then 1 to 9					
Begins to represent numbers using fingers, marks on paper or pictures					
Selects the correct numeral to represent 1 to 5, then 1 to 9, objects					
Recognises numerals 1 to 9					
Uses mathematical language in play					
Recognises groups with one, two or three objects					
Shows increased confidence with numbers by spotting errors	■		Knows that counting is a way of finding out how many		
Says the number after any number up to 9					
Uses developing ideas and methods to solve practical problems					
Compares two groups of objects, saying when they have the same number					
Shows an interest in number problems					
Separates a group of three or four objects in different ways, beginning to recognise that the total is still the same					

Sometimes shows confidence and offers solution to problems		
Uses own methods to solve a problem		
EARLY LEARNING GOAL		
In practical activities and discussion begins to use vocabulary involved in adding and subtracting	■	Combines groups of objects and shows an interest in the size of the resulting group
	■	Removes objects from a group and shows an interest in the size of the resulting group
	■	Talks about the result of combining groups of objects and removing objects from a group
	■	Describes the actions and results of combining groups and removing objects from groups, using words associated with mathematics such as 'add', 'take away', 'more', 'fewer', and 'greater'
Compares two groups of objects, saying when they have the same number	■	Counts the number of objects in each of two groups in order to find out whether they have the same number of objects
EARLY LEARNING GOAL		
Uses language such as 'more' or 'less' to compare two numbers	■	Shows interest in comparing the number of objects in two groups
	■	Counts two groups of objects in order to find out which group has more objects
	■	Talks about the number of objects in each of two groups, using words like 'more', 'greater', 'fewer' to compare the number of objects in the groups

Says with confidence the number that is one more than a given number	■ Is familiar with rhymes in which objects are removed one by one, such as *Five currant buns* ■ Takes one object away from a group of objects, adds one object to a group of objects and counts the resulting number of objects ■ Can add one or take one away from a number between 1 and 10 without using objects to do so
EARLY LEARNING GOAL **Finds one more or one less than a number from one to ten**	■ Say with confidence the number that is one less than a given number
Separates a group of three or four objects in different ways, beginning to recognise that the total is still the same	
Finds the total number of items in two groups by counting all of them	
EARLY LEARNING GOAL **Begins to relate addition to combining two groups of objects and subtraction to 'taking away'**	■ Uses counting to find out how many items there are in two groups when the number of items in the first group is known ■ Uses counting to find out how many objects are left in a group when a particular number of objects have been removed

Orders two items by weight or capacity	■ Uses words that are involved in measurement of amount such as heavy, light, full, empty ■ Uses sense to compare weight and volume ■ Uses tools to measure amount for example, scales for weight, measuring jugs for volume
EARLY LEARNING GOAL **Uses language such as 'greater', 'smaller', 'heavier' or 'lighter' to compare quantities**	
Shows an interest in shape and space by playing with shapes or making arrangements with objects	
Shows an interest by sustained construction activity or by talking about shapes or arrangements	■ Recognises patterns in the environment, for example on wrapping paper and wallpaper
Orders two or three items by length	■ In play/craft activities, copies the pattern made by an adult, such as threading beads in a particular order ■ Creates own patterns ■ Talks about the features of familiar patterns - those in the environment and also patterns s/he has made
EARLY LEARNING GOAL **Talks about, recognises and recreates simple patterns**	
Shows an interest in shape and space by playing with shapes or making arrangements with objects	■ Handles two and three dimensional shapes
Show an awareness of similarities in shapes in the environment	

Shows an interest by sustained construction activity or by talking about shapes or arrangements		
Begins to talk about the shapes of everyday objects		
Matches some shapes by recognising similarities and orientation		
Shows curiosity and observation by talking about shapes, how they are the same or why some are different		
Selects a particular named shape	■	Recognises and names an increasing range of two and three dimensional shapes
Begins to use mathematical names for "solid" 3d shapes and "flat" 2d shapes and mathematical terms to describe shapes		
Shows awareness of symmetry		
Uses language such as 'circle' to describe the shapes of solids and flat shapes		
Uses size language such as "big" and "little"	■ ■	Shows an interest in the difference in size between objects Makes comparisons between the size of one object and another
Orders two items by length or height	■	Uses comparative words such as bigger, smaller, longer, shorter to compare the size of objects

EARLY LEARNING GOAL

EARLY LEARNING GOAL

Uses language such as 'bigger' to describe the size of solids and flat shapes

	Decides where to position objects	Moves objects to a specified position	Compares the position of two objects
Observes and uses positional language			
Finds items from positional/directional clues	■	■	■
Describes a simple journey			
Instructs a programmable toy			

EARLY LEARNING GOAL

Uses everyday words to describe position

Uses shapes appropriately for tasks

Sustains interest for a length of time on a pre-decided construction or arrangement

Uses appropriate shapes to make representational models or more elaborate pictures

Chooses suitable components to make a particular model

Adapts shapes or cuts material to size

EARLY LEARNING GOAL

Uses developing ideas and methods to solve practical problems

Knowledge & understanding of the world

STEPPING STONES	SMALLER STAGES IN PROGRESS	DATE ACHIEVED
Shows curiosity and interest by facial expression, movement or sound		
Shows curiosity, observes and manipulates objects		
EARLY LEARNING GOAL **Investigates objects and materials by using all of her/his senses as appropriate**	■ Uses a single sense to investigate ■ Uses a combination of senses to investigate ■ Describes the outcomes of using senses to investigate	
Describes simple features of objects and events	■ Shows interest in an increasing range of living things, objects and events	
Examines objects and living things to find out more about them		
EARLY LEARNING GOAL **Finds out about, and identifies some features of living things, objects and events she/he observes**		
Explores objects		
Sorts objects by one function		
Notices and comment on patterns		
Shows an awareness of change	■ Recognises similarities, differences, patterns and change when attention is drawn to them by others	

EARLY LEARNING GOAL

Looks closely at similarities, differences, patterns and change

- Uses several features in order to make comparisons

Shows an interest in why things happen and how things work

Talks about what is seen and what is happening

EARLY LEARNING GOAL

Asks questions about why things happen and how things work

- Asks questions about specific objects and events
- Asks questions about general environment
- Follows up explanations with further questions
- Uses other people to find answers to questions
- Uses recorded material to find answers to questions

Investigates construction materials

Joins construction pieces together to build and balance

- Experiments with resources to see how they behave
- Experiments with resources to see what it is possible to do with them

Constructs with a purpose in mind

EARLY LEARNING GOAL

Builds and constructs with a wide range of objects, selecting appropriate resources, and adapting her/his work where necessary

- Plans how she/he will construct with resources

Realises tools can be used for a purpose

Begins to try out a range of tools and techniques safely	■ Finds out how tools work ■ Tries to use tools	
Uses simple tools and techniques competently and appropriately	■ Uses tools proficiently ■ Recognises which tool is best for a particular task	
Selects tools and techniques that she/he needs to shape, assemble and join materials she/he is using		EARLY LEARNING GOAL
Shows an interest in ICT		
Knows how to operate simple equipment	■ Follows instructions on how to operate simple equipment	
Completes a simple programme on the computer and/or performs simple functions on ICT apparatus		
Finds out about and identifies the uses of everyday technology and use ICT and programmable toys to support her/his learning	■ Knows about the part played by technological apparatus and computers in everyday life ■ Undertakes activities to find out about the part played by technological apparatus and computers in everyday life.	EARLY LEARNING GOAL
Remembers and talks about significant things that have happened to her/him		
Shows an interest in the lives of people familiar to her/him		
Begins to differentiate between past and present		

EARLY LEARNING GOAL

Finds out about past and present events in her/his life and the lives of her/his family and other people she/he knows

Shows an interest in the world in which she/he lives

Comments and asks questions about where she/he lives and the natural world

■ Wants to know about the past and present of others

EARLY LEARNING GOAL

Observes, finds out about, and identifies features in the place where she/he lives and the natural world

Shows an interest in the world in which she/he lives

■ Describes made and natural features in the environment

■ Asks questions about made and natural features in the environment

Notices differences between features of the local environment

■ Notices and describes events in the pre-school setting

■ Compares objects and events in the pre-school setting with those at home

EARLY LEARNING GOAL

Finds out about her/his environment, and talks about features she/he likes and dislikes

■ Identifies liked and disliked aspects of pre-school environment

■ Talks about the wider local environment beyond home and pre-school setting

■ Identifies liked and disliked aspects of the wider environment.

Expresses feelings about a significant personal event

Describes significant events for family or friends

Gains an awareness of the cultures and beliefs of others

- Shows interest in special events in the lives of others
- Participates willingly in experiences connected with the food, artefacts and events relevant to a range of cultures and beliefs
- Talks about the food, artefacts and events relevant to a range of cultures and beliefs
- Asks questions about the food, artefacts and events which are part of a range of cultures and beliefs

Begins to know about her/his own culture and beliefs and those of other people

Physical development

STEPPING STONES	SMALLER STAGES IN PROGRESS	DATE ACHIEVED
Moves spontaneously within available space		
Responds to rhythm, music and story by means of gesture and movement		
Can stop		
Moves freely with pleasure and confidence		
Moves in a range of ways, such as slithering, shuffling, rolling, crawling, walking, running, jumping, skipping, sliding and hopping		
Uses movement to express feelings		

Adjusts speed or changes direction to avoid obstacles

Negotiates space successfully when playing racing and chasing games with other children

Goes backwards and sideways as well as forwards

Experiments with different ways of moving

Initiates new combinations of movement and gesture in order to express and respond to feelings, ideas and experiences

Jumps off an object and lands appropriately

Moves with confidence, imagination and in safety

Manages body to create intended movements

Combines and repeats a range of movements

Sits up, stands up and balances on various parts of the body

Manipulates materials and objects by picking up, releasing, arranging, threading and posting them

Shows increasing control over clothing and fastenings

Moves with control and co-ordination

Manages body to create intended movements

EARLY LEARNING GOAL

EARLY LEARNING GOAL

Mounts stairs, steps or climbing equipment using alternate feet

- Uses clambering movements to travel up and over climbing equipment
- Experiments with ways to use equipment

EARLY LEARNING GOAL

Travels around, under, over and through balancing and climbing equipment

Negotiates an appropriate pathway when walking, running or using a wheelchair or other mobility aids, both indoors and outdoors

Judges body space in relation to spaces available when fitting into confined spaces or negotiating holes and boundaries

Shows respect for other children's personal space when playing among them

Perseveres in repeating some actions/attempts when developing a new skill

Collaborates in devising and sharing tasks, including those which involve accepting rules

Moves body position as necessary

Shows a clear and consistent preference for the left or right hand

Shows awareness of space, of themselves and of others

EARLY LEARNING GOAL

Shows awareness of own needs with regard to eating, sleeping and hygiene

Often needs adult support to meet these needs

Shows awareness of a range of healthy practices with regard to eating, sleeping and hygiene

Shows some understanding that good practices with regard to exercise, eating, sleeping and hygiene can contribute to good health

- Can give some reasons why it is necessary to have rest and sleep
- Can give some reasons why food is important
- Can give some reasons why some foods make special contributions to health
- Can give some reasons why exercise is important for health
- Can give some reasons why hygiene is necessary

EARLY LEARNING GOAL

Recognises the importance of keeping healthy and those things which contribute to this

Observes the effects of activity on her/his body

EARLY LEARNING GOAL

Recognises changes that happen to her/his bodies when she/he is active

- Talks about these changes
- Talks about why they happen

Operates equipment by means of pushing and pulling movements

Constructs with large materials such as cartons, long lengths of fabric and planks

Shows increasing control in using equipment for climbing, scrambling, sliding and swinging

Uses increasing control over an object by touching, pushing, patting, throwing, catching or kicking it			
Retrieves, collects and catches objects			
Uses a range of small and large equipment			
EARLY LEARNING GOAL			
Engages in activities requiring hand-eye coordination			
Uses one-handed tools and equipment			
Demonstrates increasing skill and control in the use of mark-making implements, blocks, construction sets and 'small world' activities			
Understands that equipment and tools have to be used safely			
Explores malleable materials by patting, stroking, poking, squeezing, pinching and twisting them			
Manipulates materials to achieve a planned effect			
Uses simple tools to effect changes to the materials			
Shows understanding of how to transport and store equipment safely			
Practises some appropriate safety measures without direct supervision			
EARLY LEARNING GOAL			

EARLY LEARNING GOAL

Handles tools, objects, construction and malleable materials safely and with increasing control

Creative development

STEPPING STONES	SMALLER STAGES IN PROGRESS	DATE ACHIEVED
Begins to differentiate colours		
Uses her/his body to explore texture and space		
Makes three-dimensional structures		
Differentiates marks and movements on paper		
Begins to describe the texture of things		
Uses lines to enclose a space, then begins to use these shapes to represent objects		
Begins to construct, stacking blocks vertically and horizontally, making enclosures and creating spaces		
Explores what happens when she/he mixes colours		
Understands that different media can be combined		
Makes constructions, collages, paintings, drawings and dances		

Uses ideas involving fitting, overlapping, in, out, enclosure, grids and sun-like shapes	
Chooses particular colours to use for a purpose	
Experiments to create different textures	
Works creatively on a large or small scale	
Explores colour, texture, shape, form and space in two and three dimensions	EARLY LEARNING GOAL
Joins in favourite songs	
Shows an interest in the way musical instruments sound	
Responds to sound with body movement	
Enjoys joining in with dancing and ring games	
Sings a few simple, familiar songs	
Sings to herself/himself and makes up simple songs	
Taps out simple repeated rhythms and makes some up	
Explores and learns how sounds can be changed	
Imitates and creates movement in response to music	
Begins to build a repertoire of songs	

Explores the different sounds of instruments									
Begins to move rhythmically									
Recognises and explores how sounds can be changed, sings simple songs from memory, recognises repeated sounds and sound patterns and matches movements to music									
Pretends that one object represents another, especially when objects have characteristics in common									
Notices what adults do, imitating what is observed and then doing it spontaneously when the adult is not there									
Uses one object to represent another, even when the objects have few characteristics in common									
Uses available resources to create props to support role play									
Develops a repertoire of actions by putting a sequence of movements together									
Enjoys stories based on themselves and people and places they know well									
Engages in imaginative and role play based on own first-hand experiences									
Introduces a story line or narrative into her/his play									

EARLY LEARNING GOAL

Plays alongside other children who are engaged in the same theme		
Plays cooperatively as part of a group to act out a narrative		
Uses her/his imagination in art and design, music, dance, imaginative and role play and stories		
EARLY LEARNING GOAL		
Shows an interest in what she/he sees, hears, smells, touches and feels		
Further explores an experience using a range of senses		
Makes comparisons	■	Describes what can see, hear, smell, touch and feel
Responds in a variety of ways to what she/he sees, hears, smells, touches and feels		
EARLY LEARNING GOAL		
Uses body language, gestures, facial expression or words to indicate personal satisfaction or frustration		
Begins to use representation as a means of communication		
Describes experiences and past actions using a widening range of materials		

	Tries to capture experiences with music, dance, paint and other materials or words	■ Tries to capture experiences and responses with music
		■ Tries to capture experiences and responses with dance
		■ Tries to capture experiences and responses with paint and other materials
		■ Tries to capture experiences and responses with words
	Develops preferences for forms of expression	
	Talks about personal intentions, describing what she/he was trying to do	
	Responds to comments and questions entering into dialogue about her/his creations	
	Expresses and communicates her/his ideas, thoughts and feelings by using a widening range of materials, suitable tools, imaginative and role play, movement, designing and making and a variety of songs and musical instruments	

EARLY LEARNING GOAL

PARENT'S SIGNATURE _____ DATE _____

Appendix 5 - RECORD OF ACHIEVEMENT

NAME OF THE CHILD:

Area of learning and development	Stage of progress achieved	Date
Personal, social and emotional development		
Communication, language and literacy		
Mathematical development		
Knowledge and understanding of the world		
Creative development		
Physical development		

PARENT'S SIGNATURE

DATE

Appendix 6 - INDIVIDUAL LEARNING PLAN

CHILDS NAME: CHILDS AGE:

NAME OF KEYWORKER:

DATE OF PLAN: DATE FOR REVIEW:

TARGET	STRATEGIES TO BE USED	DATE	COMMENTS

PARENT'S SIGNATURE

DATE

Appendix 7 - OTHER PUBLICATIONS BY THE PRE-SCHOOL LEARNING ALLIANCE

Play activities

Glueing
Make believe play
Sand and water
Clay and dough
Wood play
Books and stories
Paint and print

Learn through play

Science through play
Technology through play
Shapes and colours through play
Music through play
Language through play
Physical development through play
Time and place through play

Learning in pre-school: planning a curriculum for the under-fives

Early learning goals resource pack

The role of adults

Equal chances

Inclusion in pre-school settings

Parent and toddler groups - self-assessment for good practice

Running a parent and toddler pre-school

Play and learning for under threes

Children with special needs in pre-school

Behaviour in pre-school groups

What do we mean by maths?

Business and management

Accident record book

Accident prevention and first aid

Accounts book

Confidential incident record

Pre-school prospectus

Medication record book

Register

Pre-schools as employers

Pre-school committees and constitution

Management in pre-schools

The role of the Special Educational Needs Co-ordinator (SENCO) in pre-school settings

---

A complete list of Pre-school Learning Alliance publications and teaching resources is available by sending a SAE to:

**Pre-school Learning Alliance
69 King's Cross Road
London
WC1X 9LL**

Publications may also be purchased from the Alliance website:
www.pre-school.org.uk
